MY BEST FRIEND

a pet-owners journal

A pet is a special friend, a big
responsibility, and a lot of fun.
Use this journal to record your pets
changes, accomplishments and all those
memorable moments you share together.
There are places to keep important
information about your new best friend,
as well as areas for photographs,
animal tips and cool Pet-Toids™.
This journal will be something for
you to enjoy for years to come.

The contents of this pet-owner's journal have been reviewed and checked for accuracy by veterinary professionals. However, the authors, reviewers and publisher disclaim all responsibility arising from any adverse effects or results that occur or might occur as a result of the inappropriate application of any of the information contained in this publication. If you have a question or concern about the appropriateness or application of the information described in this journal, consult your veterinarian.

The Pet-Tips and Pet-Toids™ contained in this journal have been supplied by numerous sources including, but not limited to, the American Animal Hospital Association (website www.healthypet.com) and Jeffrey Werber, DVM (host of Animal Planet's, "Petcetera," and Pet Expert on CBS-TV, Los Angeles). Some information contained herein has come from anonymous and second—or third—hand sources. By its very nature, some of the data contained herein is particularly susceptible to folklore and rumor. While we have attempted to eliminate incorrect entries, the Publisher and Author will not accept responsibility or liability for any views/claims/rumours/errors that appear herein.

Credits:

Written by Ron Solomon

Design by Sheila Schatz and Swingset Press, LLC

This is my new best friend.

_____
(pet name)

_____
(date)

MY PHOTO HERE

PET PHOTO HERE

I know (s)he will need to be taken good care of and I promise to do that.

_____
(my name)

PAGE 1

My Best Friend Is Finally Here!

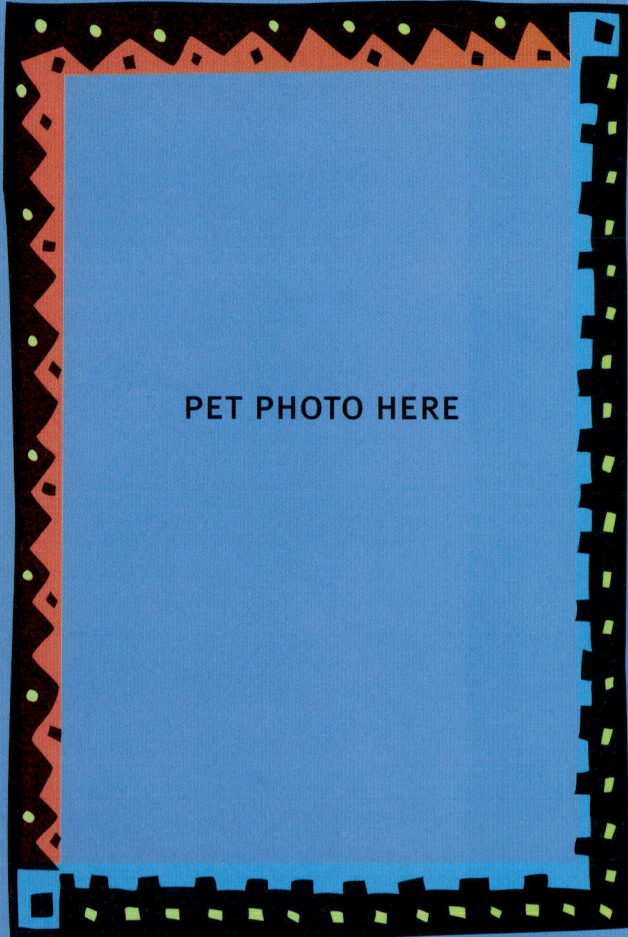

PET PHOTO HERE

THIS IS A PICTURE OF MY BEST FRIEND AND ME AT HOME ON THE FIRST DAY.

HERE IS SOME PERSONAL INFORMATION ABOUT MY BEST FRIEND ON THE DATE OF ARRIVAL:

ARRIVAL DATE:_____

WHERE MY BEST FRIEND IS FROM:_____

_____

_____

AGE:_____

DATE OF BIRTH:_____

BREED/GENUS:_____

_____

LENGTH:_____

WEIGHT:_____

HEIGHT:_____

COLOR OF COAT/SCALES/FEATHERS:_____

_____

COLOR OF EYES:_____

DISTINGUISHING MARKS:_____

_____

_____

_____

I'LL NEVER FORGET THE DAY MY BEST FRIEND ARRIVED. . .

_____

_____

_____

_____

_____

_____

_____

_____

_____

_____

_____

_____

_____

_____

_____

_____

_____

_____

Pet-Toid™

MORE THAN PEOPLE SURVIVED THE TITANIC: TWO DOGS LIVED THROUGH IT, AS WELL! A POMERANIAN AND A PEKINESE ESCAPED ON TWO OF THE FIRST LIFEBOATS. DO YOU THINK THEY COULD GET LEONARDO DI COLLIE TO DO THE MOVIE?

Z Z Z Z Z

Pet Tips: Showing Thanks For Our Pets

We love our pets more than ever. In fact, they're kind of like having children of your own! Pets entertain us, make us laugh, and love us unconditionally. What can we do to show them our thanks? Here's a list of things you can do to show your pet how much you care.

1 Spend quality time with your pet by going for walks, hanging out in the back yard, playing games with their favorite toys, or snuggling with them as you watch TV or read a book.

2 Update your pet's identification tags! Many of us move or change phone numbers but forget to update the tags. It's scary to think about, but if your pet gets lost, it's one of the best tools to ensure a safe return.

3 Always get your pet immediate veterinary care if you suspect that something is wrong. If you don't have a solid relationship with your veterinarian, work on that for the sake of your pet. Remember, a good veterinarian is your greatest ally.

4 Protect your pet from home hazards and from extremes of weather. They cannot protect themselves.

5 Feed your pet healthy food intended for them, not potato chips, cookies, and other fatty human foods.

HERE'S A LIST OF THE COOL STUFF MY BEST FRIEND GOT
WHEN (S)HE ARRIVED. . .

Gift	Gift Giver

Cool Gifts For My Best Friend!

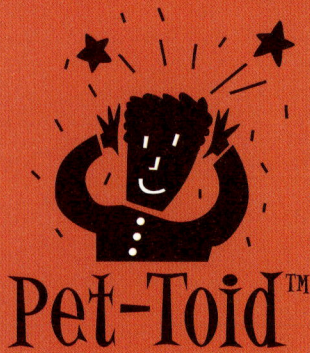

Pet-Toid™

WE'VE ALL HEARD OF
WATCHDOGS, BUT HOW
ABOUT WATCHCATS?
BUDDHIST MONKS USED
TO KEEP SIAMESE CATS
TO PROTECT THEIR PLACES
OF WORSHIP. IF SOMEONE
BROKE IN, THE CATS WOULD
"MEOW" THE ALARM.

This is where my best friend sleeps...

PLACE PHOTO HERE

WHERE ELSE DOES (S)HE LIKE TO SLEEP?_____

_____

WHAT DO YOU THINK YOUR BEST FRIEND DREAMS ABOUT?_____

_____

_____

DOES YOUR BEST FRIEND SNORE?

☐ NEVER

☐ A LITTLE

☐ THE WALLS SHAKE!

These are my best friend's
Paw / Hoof / Claw / Scale / Fin Prints

Date:_____ Age:_____

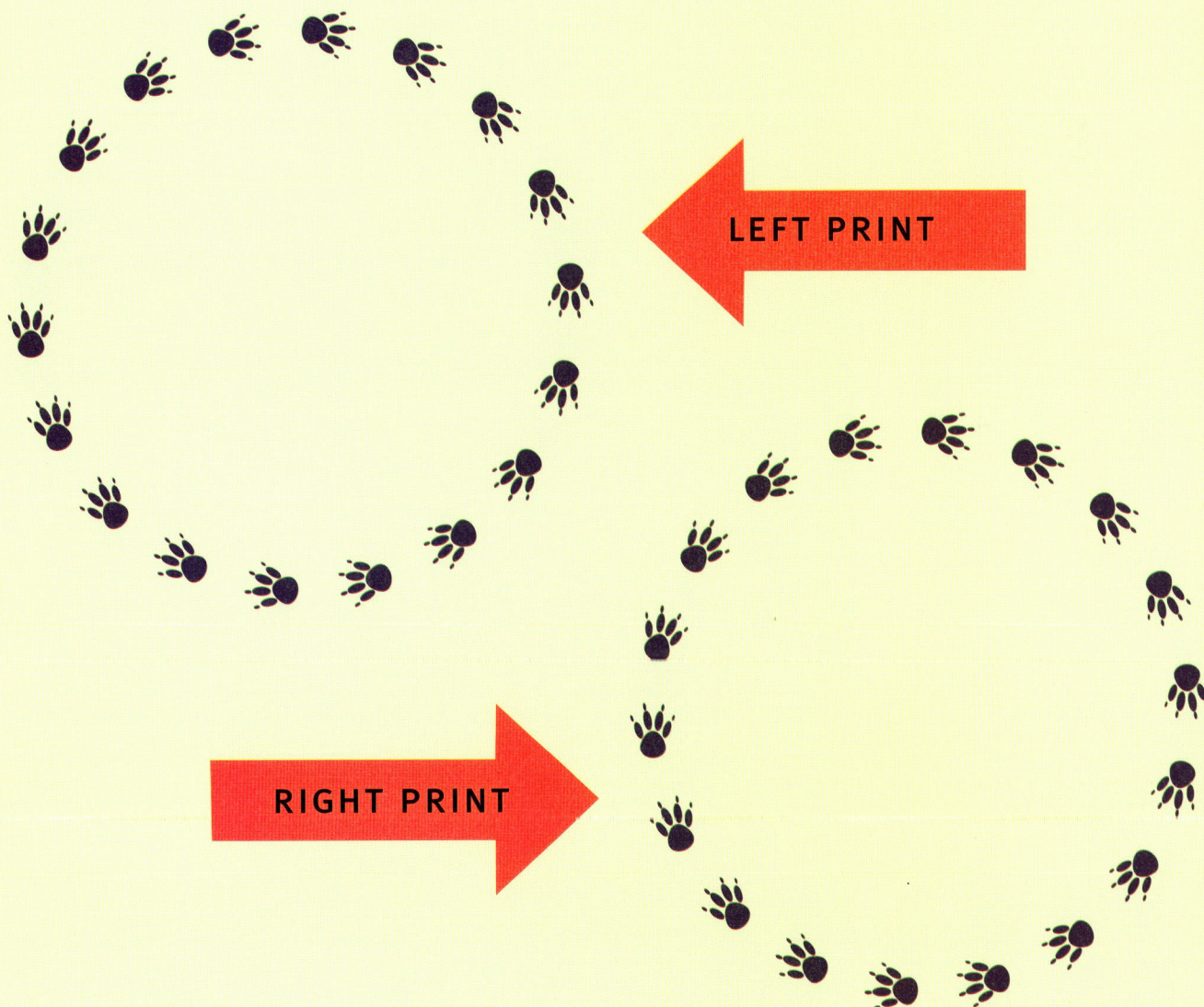

LEFT PRINT

RIGHT PRINT

PLEASE NOTE:

ANIMAL PRINTS TO BE DONE ONLY WITH ADULT SUPERVISION.

PLEASE BE SURE TO USE ONLY WATERCOLORS OR NON-TOXIC INK.

Pet Tips: Keep Your Pet Healthy and Happy!

As a responsible pet owner, you can take a few simple steps that will go a long way toward keeping your pet healthy and happy. Here are some practical tips that can ensure your pet's health and happiness.

1 Make your home a safe environment. Pet proofing can lower the risk of a serious pet accident occurring. A pet owner needs to be aware of several potential dangers. Poisons in the home that can seriously injure your pet include some kinds of house plants (philodendron, hyacinth, and mistletoe), pesticides, and medications. Also, low electrical cords are extremely hazardous when chewed.

2 Make sure your pet receives a complete check-up. "With wellness and preventive medicine becoming such an integral part of our pets' health, annual physical exams are more important than ever," says Dr. Jeff Werber, host of Animal Planet's, "Petcetera" and pet expert for CBS-TV, Los Angeles. "With costs of quality veterinary care on the rise, early disease detection and prevention are key," he added. Your veterinarian can conduct a thorough exam that includes a lab analysis, heart check, and dental exam.

3 Design a diet and exercise plan to meet your pet's specific needs. Obesity leads to serious dog and cat health problems such as heart disease. Exercise is important, but a pet will only exercise if there is an incentive to do so. Your veterinarian will consider what stage of life your pet is in, the amount of activity your pet enjoys, and the time of year before outlining a specific plan. The right kind of food and physical activity can add to the quality of your best friend's life.

My best friend gets the best medical care...

VETERINARIAN INFORMATION

NAME: _____

ADDRESS: _____

_____

PHONE: _____

EMERGENCY INFORMATION

EMERGENCY PHONE: _____

LICENSE NUMBER: _____

LOCAL ASPCA: _____

OTHER NUMBERS: _____

_____

MEDICAL INFORMATION

ALLERGIES: _____

MEDICATIONS: _____

SPADE/NEUTERED: _____

VETERINARIAN'S PHOTO HERE

Pet-Toid™

THE WHALE SHARK IS THE

LARGEST FISH IN THE WORLD.

THE LONGEST ONE WAS

41 $\frac{1}{2}$ FEET LONG,

23 FEET AROUND AND

WEIGHED NEARLY 20 TONS!

HEY, MOM, CAN I

KEEP IT IN THE POOL?

CAN I, HUH?

_____

My Best Friend's

VACCINATION

	WEEKS	WEEKS	WEEKS	WEEKS	WEEKS	1 YEAR	2 YEARS	3 YEARS	4 YEARS	5 YEARS
DOGS										
DISTEMPER										
ADENOVIRUS										
LEPTOSPIROSIS										
PARAINFLUENZA										
PARVOVIRUS										
CORONAVIRUS										
BORDETELLA										
LYME										
CATS										
PANLEUKOPENIA										
RHINOTRACHEITIS										
CALICIVIRUS										
FELINE LEUKEMIA										
FIP										
DOGS & CATS										
RABIES										
HEARTWORM										
PARASITE CHECK										
	DATE	DATE	DATE	DATE	DATE	DATE	DATE	DATE	DATE	DATE

Medical Records

RECORD

6 YEARS	7 YEARS	8 YEARS	9 YEARS	10 YEARS	11 YEARS	12 YEARS	13 YEARS	14 YEARS	15 YEARS
DATE	DATE	DATE	DATE	DATE	DATE	DATE	DATE	DATE	DATE

Pet Tips: Chocolate is Dangerous for Pets

If you give chocolate to loved ones, you could end up hurting them very badly. That is, if the loved ones are your pets.

1 EVEN SMALL AMOUNTS OF THEOBROMINE, AN INGREDIENT IN CHOCOLATE, CAN CAUSE VOMITING AND RESTLESSNESS IN PETS. LARGER DOSES CAN BE FATAL (WHICH MEANS THEY COULD DIE). WHILE MOST PET OWNERS THINK DOGS MAY ONLY GET AN UPSET STOMACH AFTER EATING A LARGE AMOUNT OF CHOCOLATE, NOT MANY PEOPLE REALIZE IT'S ACTUALLY POISONOUS!

2 ESTIMATES OF THE SMALLEST AMOUNTS THAT CAN BE FATAL ARE:

▸ 4 TO 10 OUNCES OF MILK CHOCOLATE (THAT'S ABOUT THE SIZE OF A LARGE CANDYBAR) OR $1/2$ TO 1 OUNCE OF BAKING CHOCOLATE FOR SMALL DOGS, SUCH AS CHIHUAHUAS AND TOY POODLES.

▸ 1 TO $1\,1/2$ POUNDS OF MILK CHOCOLATE OR 2 TO 3 OUNCES OF BAKING CHOCOLATE FOR MEDIUM-SIZED DOGS, LIKE COCKER SPANIELS AND DACHSHUNDS.

▸ 2 TO $4\,1/2$ POUNDS OF MILK CHOCOLATE OR 4 TO 8 OUNCES OF BAKING CHOCOLATE FOR LARGE DOGS, INCLUDING COLLIES AND LABRADOR RETRIEVERS.

3 CATS HAVE MUCH DIFFERENT EATING HABITS AND SELDOM ARE POISONED BY CHOCOLATE. BUT, YOU SHOULD STILL ASK YOUR VETERINARIAN BEFORE YOU GIVE THEM ANY.

4 WHILE A VERY SMALL AMOUNT OF CHOCOLATE MAY NOT HARM SOME DOGS, IT'S SAFEST TO AVOID GIVING IT TO THEM AT ALL. IF ANY ACCIDENT OCCURS, A VETERINARIAN SHOULD BE CONSULTED, IMMEDIATELY!

This is where my best friend eats...

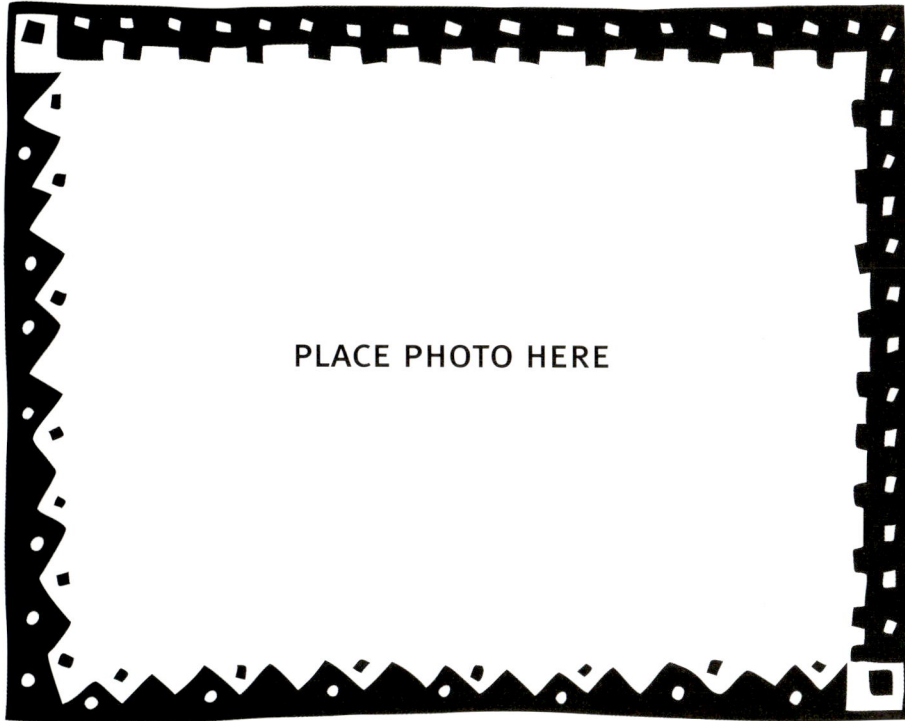

PLACE PHOTO HERE

WHAT'S YOUR PET'S FAVORITE FOOD? _____

_____

HOW OFTEN DOES YOUR BEST FRIEND EAT?

☐ ONCE A DAY   ☐ TWICE A DAY   ☐ NEVER STOPS!

WHAT KIND OF AN EATER IS YOUR PET?

☐ NEAT   ☐ KIND OF SLOPPY   ☐ KEEP A BROOM HANDY!

☐ SLOW   ☐ KIND OF FAST   ☐ WATCH YOUR FINGERS!

☐ FINICKY   ☐ LIKES MOST FOOD   ☐ (S)HE'S PART GOAT!

Pet-Toid™

IN AFRICA AND INDIA SOME PEOPLE ACTUALLY HAVE ELEPHANTS AS PETS. BUT, SINCE ELEPHANTS EAT UP TO FIVE HUNDRED POUNDS OF FOOD A DAY, YOU KIND OF WONDER WHERE THEY GET BOWLS BIG ENOUGH TO PUT IT IN!

Here are some of my best friend's peers...

FAMOUS ANIMAL MOVIE STARS: _____

_____

_____

_____

FAMOUS ANIMAL TELEVISION STARS: _____

_____

_____

PRESIDENTIAL PET(S): _____

_____

KENTUCKY DERBY WINNER: _____

_____

ANIMALS IN THE NEWS: _____

_____

_____

_____

_____

FAMOUS ANIMAL CIRCUS STARS: _____

_____

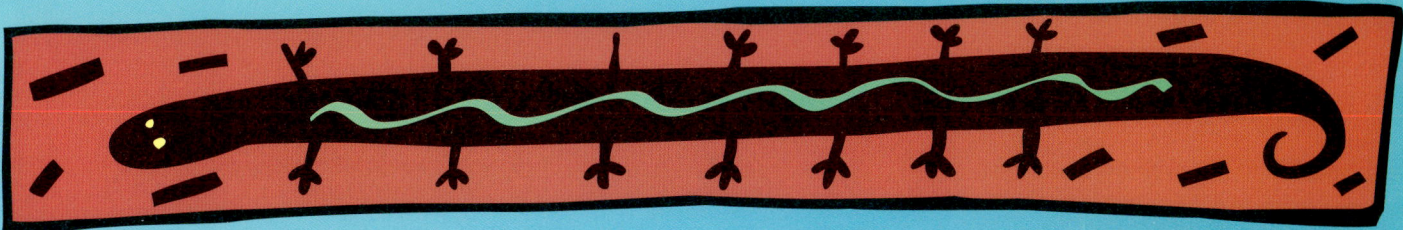

My best friend comes from a pretty big family...

MY BEST FRIEND

MY BEST FRIEND'S MOM

MY BEST FRIEND'S DAD

MY BEST FRIEND'S MATERNAL GRANDMOTHER

MY BEST FRIEND'S PATERNAL GRANDMOTHER

MY BEST FRIEND'S MATERNAL GRANDFATHER

MY BEST FRIEND'S PATERNAL GRANDFATHER

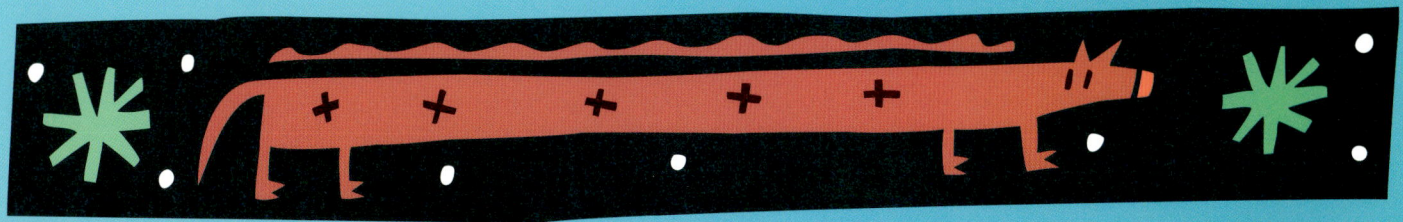

Pet Tips: The Face Lickin' Friends

If you just got a puppy, you're about to learn what your parents go through with you! Because even though dogs have been mankind's best friend for nearly 5,000 years, puppies aren't born knowing the rules. They don't know it's wrong to chew your toys, use the kitchen as a bathroom, or jump onto your bed right after taking a dip in the pool. They need you to teach them.

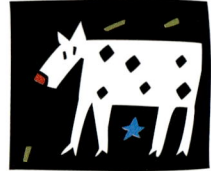

1 At your new best friend's first visit to the veterinarian (which should be on his or her first day home) ask lots of questions. Find out about important things like diet, grooming, training, housebreaking (that's teaching your dog to go to the bathroom outside) and neutering. This is all super important stuff to know as a dog owner.

2 Another thing your puppy won't know about is people. Start with simple, quiet, one-person introductions, and gradually include more people in noisier situations. Invite friends, relatives, and their pets to come over to meet and play with the pup. As soon as your veterinarian says your puppy has had the right shots, take it out as much as possible.

4 Stuff you'll need:
- COLLAR AND LEASH
- IDENTIFICATION TAGS
- A BOX, BLANKET OR PAD
- TWO BOWLS (FOR WATER AND FOOD)
- TOYS AND TREATS
- DOG FOOD

3 You'll definitely want to teach your pooch good manners. Maybe you could even take some training classes with your dog, so you both can learn. But however you decide to train your dog, remember that punishment during puppy-hood can affect good people skills. Avoid physical discipline, like swatting the pup, thumping it on the nose, or rubbing its nose in a mess.

5 Did you realize that dogs (canis familiaris) can do lots more than be great pets? The armed forces have used dogs for guard, security, and attack purposes. Police departments use patrol dogs because of their keen senses of hearing and smell. Dogs are used for herding ducks, geese, sheep and cattle. They're used as guide dogs for the blind, assistance dogs for the physically challenged and as sled dogs. Sometimes they even become famous Hollywood stars, like lassie, rin tin tin and air bud. Do you think they eat from gold bowls?

Tricks, Talents and Special Skills

COMMAND	SPECIAL SKILL

Pet-Toid™

WHILE PRESIDENT, THOMAS JEFFERSON HAD A MOCKINGBIRD NAMED DICK. JEFFERSON LET DICK TAKE FOOD FROM HIS LIPS, RIDE ON HIS SHOULDER, AND WHEN JEFFERSON WENT UPSTAIRS, DICK HOPPED RIGHT UP WITH HIM. DO YOU THINK THE FIRST TIME DICK SAW HIS NEW MASTER HE SAID, "I TAWT I TAW A PWESIDENT?!"

The Inside Scoop!

Why I decided on this type of animal: _____

_____

_____

_____

_____

How I picked my best friend's name: _____

_____

_____

_____

_____

Other names I considered: _____

_____

_____

_____

If I were an animal, I'd want to be: _____

_____

_____

_____

This is my best friend's first haircut...

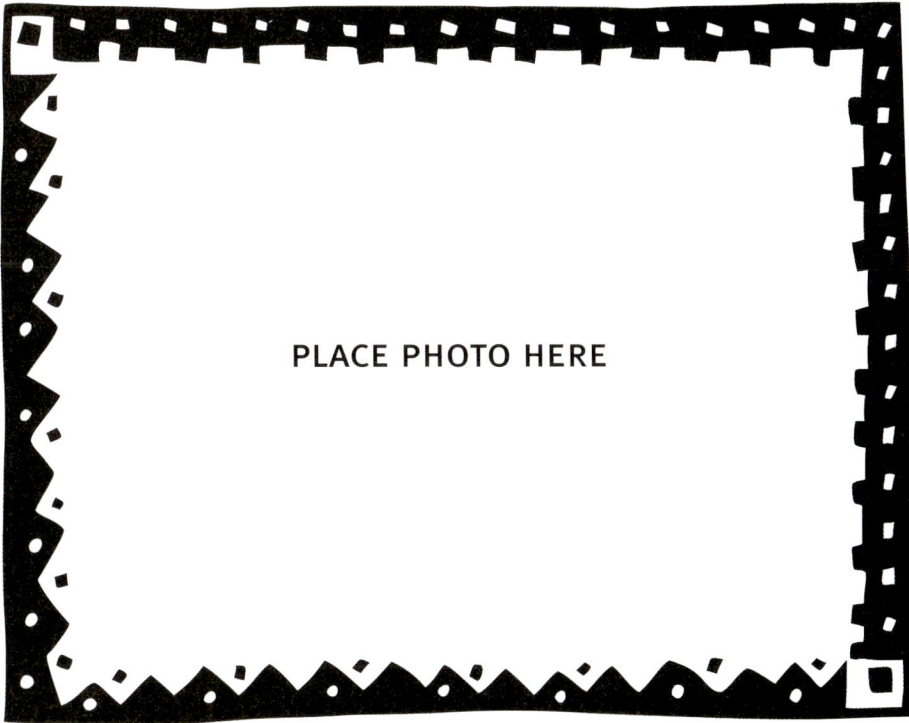

PLACE PHOTO HERE

Take it from me, it was a "hair-raising" experience.

Here's what happened...

_____

_____

_____

_____

_____

_____

_____

_____

_____

Pet Tips: Caring For Our Feline Friends

PROUD, INDEPENDENT, LOYAL AND INTELLIGENT — THESE ARE SOME OF THE WAYS CAT-OWNERS DESCRIBE THEIR PETS. ACTUALLY, MANY CAT-OWNERS FEEL LIKE THEY'RE THE PET AND THEIR CAT IS THE MASTER! AND IT'S NO WONDER, WHEN IT COMES TO BEING PETS, MOST CATS DON'T BEHAVE LIKE DOGS. OH, THEY'LL CUDDLE ALL RIGHT. . . WHEN THEY WANT TO. AND THEY'LL DO SOME TRICKS. . . IF THEY FEEL LIKE IT. BUT THIS SENSE OF INDEPENDENCE IS SOMETHING YOU SHOULD RESPECT — IT MAKES CATS VERY UNIQUE AS PETS. BUT THEY'RE ALSO SUPER LOYAL AND EXTREMELY LOVING.

1 DID YOU KNOW THAT 3,000 YEARS AGO IN ANCIENT EGYPT, CATS WERE THOUGHT TO BE SACRED? WELL, IT'S TRUE! THE PILGRIMS EVEN BROUGHT THEIR PET TABBIES TO AMERICA ON THE MAYFLOWER! BOOKS, STORIES AND EVEN BROADWAY PLAYS HAVE BEEN WRITTEN ABOUT CATS, AND MANY "CAT" EXPRESSIONS ARE USED BY PEOPLE WHETHER THEY HAVE ONE AS A PET, OR NOT.

2 ONE EXPRESSION YOU MAY HAVE HEARD IS, "CURIOSITY KILLED THE CAT." THIS IS A WISE SAYING BECAUSE CATS (KITTENS ESPECIALLY) WANT TO EXPLORE EVERYTHING. THAT MEANS YOU MUST "KITTENPROOF" YOUR HOME. TO SEE POSSIBLE DANGERS, PRETEND YOU'RE A KITTEN BY GETTING ON YOUR HANDS AND KNEES AND LOOKING AT THE WORLD FROM A CAT'S-EYE VIEW. WHILE CRAWLING AROUND, PUT AWAY THINGS THAT COULD BE SWALLOWED. GET YOUR PARENTS TO COVER ELECTRICAL CORDS, AND CLOSE OFF AREAS LIKE POOLS AND BALCONIES. JUST DON'T GET CARRIED AWAY AND EAT THE CAT FOOD, OKAY?

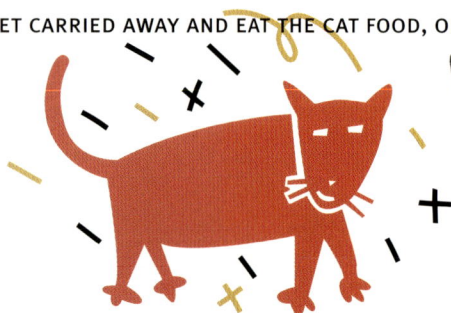

5 STUFF YOU'LL NEED:
- COLLAR AND LEASH
- IDENTIFICATION TAGS
- FOOD AND WATER BOWLS
- LITTER BOX AND CAT LITTER
- SCRATCH PADS
- CLIMBING TOYS
- A CAT CARRIER

4 CATS (CLASSIFICATION, FILIDAE) LOVE TO EAT MEAT. IN FACT, THESE CUDDLY CARNIVORES NEED A HIGH-CALORIE, HIGH-QUALITY DIET THAT'S RICH IN ANIMAL PROTEIN AND FAT. A COMBINATION OF DRY AND CANNED CAT FOODS SHOULD BE FINE, BUT IT'S A GOOD IDEA TO ASK YOUR VETERINARIAN WHAT YOUR FELINE FRIEND SHOULD EAT. AND WHATEVER THEIR DIET, A CONSTANT SUPPLY OF FRESH WATER IS ESSENTIAL.

3 ANOTHER SAYING YOU MAY HAVE HEARD IS, "CATS HAVE NINE LIVES." THIS IS NOT TRUE! WHILE CATS DO HAVE AN AMAZING SENSE OF BALANCE (SOME CATS HAVE BEEN KNOWN TO SURVIVE FORTY FOOT FALLS!), THEY ARE ANIMALS WITH ONLY ONE LIFE. IT'S YOUR JOB TO HELP KEEP YOUR CAT SAFE.

My best friend has an awesome personality!

(S)HE LOVES TO: _____

_____

_____

_____

(S)HE LIKES IT WHEN I: _____

_____

_____

_____

(S)HE ENJOYS PLAYING WITH: _____

_____

_____

_____

(S)HE GETS EXCITED WHEN: _____

_____

_____

_____

(S)HE MUST BE PART HUMAN BECAUSE: _____

_____

_____

_____

Pet-Toid™

TOBY II, A SOOTY-FAWN

ENGLISH LOP RABBIT

HAS EARS THAT ARE

OVER TWO FEET LONG AND

OVER SEVEN INCHES WIDE.

IT'S RUMORED THAT SHE

CAN HEAR A CARROT POP

OUT OF THE GROUND

FROM A MILE AWAY!

These are some of my best friend's pals...

PLACE PHOTO HERE

NAME _____

PLACE PHOTO HERE

NAME _____

Pet Tips: Caring For Your Aquatic Friends

O**N THE SURFACE IT MAY SEEM LIKE FISH ARE THE EASIEST PETS TO HAVE. AFTER ALL, THEY DON'T NEED LITTER BOXES, VACCINATIONS, OR OBEDIENCE CLASSES (AND THAT'S NOT BECAUSE THEY LIVE IN SCHOOLS). BUT DON'T BE FOOLED, YOU CAN'T JUST FILL UP A BOWL OF WATER, PLOP YOUR FISH IN AND EXPECT IT TO SURVIVE. NO WAY. THESE COLD BLOODED, AQUATIC ANIMALS HAVE SPECIAL NEEDS AND WILL DEPEND ON YOU TO KEEP THEM HEALTHY AND HAPPY.**

1 YOUR PET FISH WILL LIVE IN A SPECIAL HOME, CALLED AN AQUARIUM. THIS CONSISTS OF A FISH TANK, WATER, GRAVEL, FILTERS AND MORE. DEPENDING ON HOW MUCH TIME AND EFFORT YOU PUT INTO IT, A WELL-DESIGNED AQUARIUM WITH JUST ONE OR MORE COLORFUL FISH, CAN BE AS MUCH FUN AS WATCHING TELEVISION. . . SERIOUSLY! THE MORE YOU WATCH, THE MORE YOU'LL GET TO KNOW YOUR FISH'S PERSONALITY. FOR INSTANCE, DID YOU KNOW THAT FISH LIKE TO HIDE WHEN THEY GET NERVOUS?

2 WHEN YOU FIRST GO TO THE PET STORE TO GET YOUR NEW, FINNY FRIEND, MAKE SURE TO DISCUSS ITS CARE WITH THE STORE OWNER. BECAUSE WHATEVER FISH YOU GET WILL HAVE SPECIFIC NEEDS AS TO NUTRITION, WATER TEMPERATURE, LIGHTING AND OTHER FACTORS. THIS IS VERY IMPORTANT. DO PLENTY OF RESEARCH! READ FISH MAGAZINES AND BOOKS, AND STAY IN TOUCH WITH YOUR LOCAL PET STORE AS QUESTIONS COME UP. THERE ARE ALSO GREAT FISH-SITES ON THE WORLD WIDE WEB.

3 PLEASE MAKE SURE THE AQUARIUM IS A HEALTHY AND HAPPY PLACE. REMEMBER, YOUR FISH (LIKE ANY PET!) IS YOUR RESPONSIBILITY. THEY HAVE NO CONTROL OVER THEIR ENVIRONMENTS, SO SETTING UP YOUR AQUARIUM THE RIGHT WAY IS ESSENTIAL. PLEASE MAKE SURE TO READ WHATEVER BOOKS YOU GET AND FOLLOW THE INSTRUCTIONS OF THE PET STORE OWNER.

4 STUFF YOU'LL NEED:

- ► FISH TANK
- ► SIPHON
- ► FILTERS
- ► HOOD
- ► PUMPS, AIR STONES
- ► GRAVEL
- ► DECORATIONS
- ► FISH FOOD

Travel Tips

GOING ON TRIPS WITH YOUR PET CAN BE AWESOME. BUT, THERE ARE SOME THINGS YOU SHOULD KNOW ABOUT TRAVELING WITH AN ANIMAL...

▸ MAKE AN APPOINTMENT WITH THE VETERINARIAN BEFORE YOUR TRIP. SOME STATES AND ALL FOREIGN COUNTRIES REQUIRE CURRENT RABIES AND HEALTH CERTIFICATES.

▸ ABOUT A WEEK BEFORE A CAR TRIP, TAKE A FEW SHORT RIDES WITH YOUR PET TO GET HIM OR HER USED TO DRIVING.

▸ MAKE SURE TO KEEP YOUR PET IN CONTROL ALL THE TIME. TRIPS HAVE MANY STOPS, WHICH MEANS A LOT OF CHANCES TO GET LOST. USE YOUR LEASHES AND PET CARRIERS. ALSO, KEEP YOUR CAR WINDOWS CLOSED ENOUGH SO YOUR PET CAN'T JUMP OUT.

▸ BRING A RECORD OF YOUR PET'S IDENTIFICATION TAGS, SO THAT IF HE OR SHE SHOULD GET LOST (PERISH THE THOUGHT!), YOU CAN GIVE THE LOCAL POLICE MORE THAN HER NAME AND DESCRIPTION.

▸ NEVER LEAVE YOUR PET ALONE IN A CLOSED CAR DURING HOT WEATHER. HE OR SHE COULD GET VERY SICK, AND IN SOME CASES EVEN DIE.

▸ THERE ARE LOTS OF PET-FRIENDLY MOTELS AND HOTELS, BUT HAVE YOUR PARENTS ASK WHEN THEY MAKE RESERVATIONS. REMEMBER TO HAVE RESPECT FOR THOSE PLACES WHILE YOU'RE THERE; WALK AND PLAY WITH YOUR PET OFF THE HOTEL GROUNDS.

▸ AS SOON AS YOU GET WHERE YOU'RE GOING, GIVE YOUR PET FOOD AND WATER (SPARINGLY), PLENTY OF UNDERSTANDING, AND TONS OF PLAY AND LOVE!

Our first vacation with my best friend...

DATE OF TRIP: _____

DESTINATION: _____

REASON FOR TRIP: _____

_____

_____

BEST FRIEND'S AGE: _____

MEANS OF TRAVEL: _____

_____

PLACE PHOTO HERE

Trip Memories

DESCRIPTION OF MY TRIP WITH MY BEST FRIEND...

Pet Tips: Is That Godzilla On Your Leash?

Excuse me, there's an iguana named Iggy on your shoulder! Don't be surprised, these green, scaly, cold-blooded creatures have warmed the hearts of many pet-owners. And why not? Snakes, iguanas, and turtles are fascinating members of our world. If treated with love and care, reptiles make fantastic pets. However, our reptilian earth-mates need more than a water bowl and a day in the park playing fetch the fly! They also need heat, water and a reptile-appropriate place to live.

1 Aquariums, custom cages and home-made boxes are all good places for a reptile to call home. The easiest (and cheapest) lining for the cages of many reptiles is newspaper. Turtles need a more humid lining, such as soil mixed with peat moss. Geckos will like smooth aquarium stones in the bottom of the cage. Snakes will appreciate rocks to help them shed, and iguanas and snakes both like to have branches for climbing.

2 Reptiles depend on the air temperature to maintain their body heat. Room temperature is too cold for most reptiles, so you'll need to warm the cage as well as provide hot spots for basking (ask your veterinarian how to do this). Make sure to keep heat sources out of the cage if possible, and never place a cage or aquarium in direct sunlight without shade.

3 All reptiles (even ones from the desert) need plenty of water to survive. Besides drinking it, some need to periodically soak to keep their scaly bodies moist. Just make sure that your reptile's personal swimming area is shallow enough that he won't drown and that it is kept clean.

4
▶ The first known reptile, Hylonomus, appeared about 300 million years ago! It was about 27 inches long and had a lizard-like shape.

▶ The python is the longest reptile on record. It can grow up to 33 feet long.

▶ The heaviest living reptile is the leatherback turtle, which can get up to 1,600 lbs. in weight (that's heavier than a horse!)

This is my best friend's first bath...

PLACE PHOTO HERE

Oh what a time we had! Here's what happened. . .

_____

_____

_____

_____

_____

_____

_____

_____

_____

_____

Pet-Toid™

WHO SAYS FIREDOGS NEED TO HAVE SPOTS? MIMI, A MINIATURE POODLE FROM DANBURY, CONNECTICUT SAVED EIGHT PEOPLE'S LIVES BY LICKING THEM! IT SEEMS THEY WERE ASLEEP WHEN THEIR HOUSE CAUGHT ON FIRE, AND MIMI LICKED THEM UNTIL THEY WOKE UP.

Some of my best friend's favorite things...

FAVORITE TOY
(PUT PHOTO OR DRAWING HERE)

FAVORITE CHEWY
(PUT PHOTO OR DRAWING HERE)

FAVORITE FOOD
(PUT PHOTO OR DRAWING HERE)

FAVORITE PLACE TO HANG-OUT...

_____
_____
_____

FAVORITE PLACE TO PLAY...

_____
_____
_____
_____

OTHER FAVORITE THINGS...

_____
_____
_____
_____

Pet Tips: Gerbils and Hamsters and Mice, Oh My!

WHILE A LOT OF PEOPLE WILL SCREAM, "EEK!" AND JUMP ONTO A CHAIR AT THE SIGHT OF A MOUSE, THERE ARE OTHERS WHO WILL LOVINGLY SCOOP THESE LITTLE GUYS UP AND NUZZLE NOSES WITH THEM. ACTUALLY, MICE, HAMSTERS, GERBILS AND GUINEA PIGS ARE AMONG THE MOST POPULAR PETS AROUND!

1 BELIEVE IT OR NOT, THERE ARE OVER 2,000 DIFFERENT KINDS OF RODENTS. AND ALTHOUGH THEY LOOK AND ACT VERY DIFFERENTLY, RODENTS HAVE CERTAIN THINGS IN COMMON. FIRST OFF, THEY ARE ALL GNAWING ANIMALS. THEY ARE MOSTLY SMALL — ALTHOUGH THE SOUTH AND CENTRAL AMERICAN CAPYBARA, CAN GROW UP TO BE 110 POUNDS (THAT'S THE SIZE OF A LARGE GERMAN SHEPHERD!) AND MANY RODENTS ARE NOCTURNAL (WHICH MEANS THEY SLEEP DURING THE DAY, AND PLAY AT NIGHT.)

2 OF MOST RODENT FEEDS AVAILABLE, ONLY THE PELLETED, COMPLETE DIETS SHOULD BE USED AS PRIMARY DIETS. THE STANDARD PELLETED, COMPLETE DIETS MAY BE FED TO THE OLD WORLD RODENTS: HAMSTERS, GERBILS, MICE, AND RATS. HAVING FRESH WATER AVAILABLE AT ALL TIMES IS CRITICAL, AS MANY PET RODENTS THAT SEEM "SICK" ARE REALLY JUST DEHYDRATED. WATER SHOULD BE GIVEN IN BOTTLES WITH METAL SIPPER TUBES (HAMSTERS MAY GNAW OR BREAK PLASTIC OR GLASS TUBES.)

3 CHECK OUT ALL THESE DIFFERENT KINDS OF RODENTS (BUT DON'T TRY TO GET ALL OF THEM FOR PETS!): BEAVERS, PRAIRIE DOGS, DEER MICE, PLAINS POCKET GOPHERS, GROUNDHOGS (WOODCHUCKS), DOMESTIC GUINEA PIGS, GOLDEN HAMSTERS, KANGAROO RATS, POCKET GOPHERS, NORTH AMERICAN PORCUPINES, SPRINGHARES, AMERICAN OR EASTERN GRAY SQUIRRELS, EASTERN RED SQUIRRELS, NORTHERN FLYING SQUIRRELS, GERBILS, HOUSE MICE, AND BLACK RATS.

Pet-Toid™

SINCE 1957,

7 DOGS, 2 CHIMPS, AND

5 MONKEYS HAVE TAKEN

FLIGHTS INTO OUTER SPACE.

SO WHEN YOUR PET

DOESN'T COME WHEN

YOU CALL, MAYBE IT'S

NOT A HEARING PROBLEM;

MAYBE HE OR SHE IS

JUST BEING SPACEY.

This is my best friend wearing clothes...

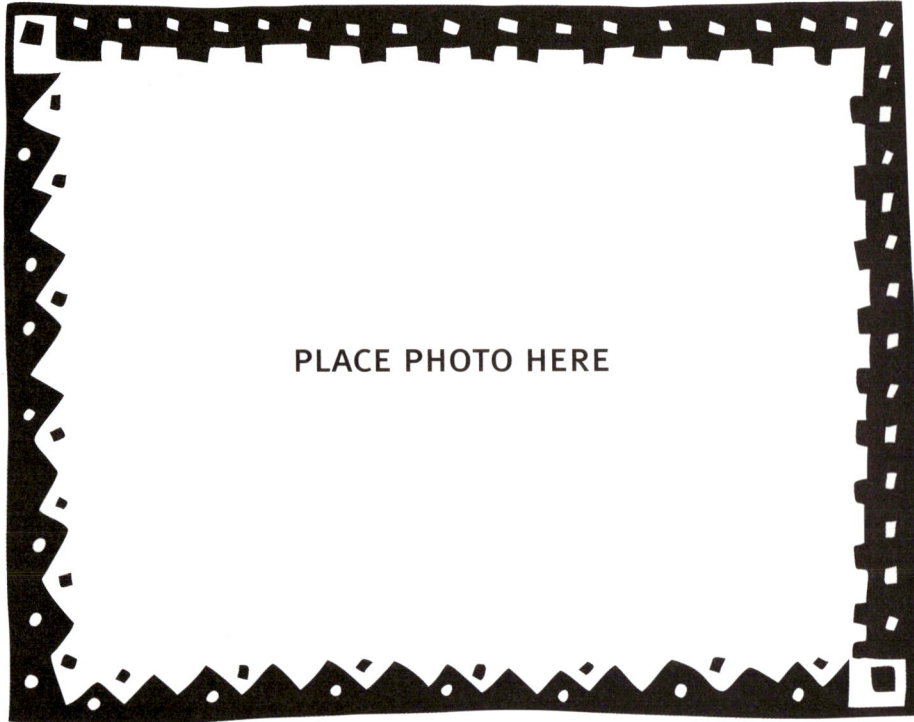

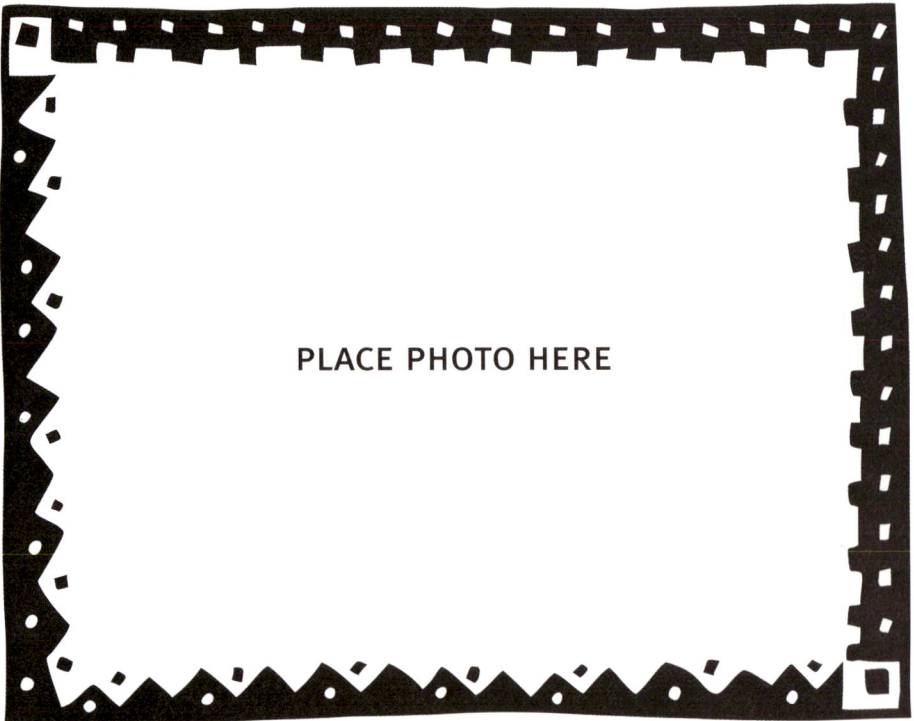

PLACE PHOTO HERE

PLACE PHOTO HERE

Pet Tips: Who Needs the School Bus, I've Got A Horse!

Taking care of a pet horse, and that includes properly feeding, exercising, boarding, grooming and keeping her healthy, is an expensive and involved job. But it's definitely worth the work, because even though you can't snuggle on the sofa to watch TV with your horse, you definitely can't go for a fun ride on your goldfish!

1 Horses (equus caballus) are vegetarians and are one of the few mammals that were adapted for running. Over time, horses have worked and played with humans beings in transportation, farming, police work, and sports. As pets, they're fun for rodeos, show riding, and even simple trail riding. And because they're so intelligent, loyal and loving, horses make great friends!

2 Here are some tips for making riding safe and comfortable:
► A well fitting and sturdy riding helmet should always be worn.
► Always wear long pants. Jeans are great for walking, but may not be great for riding because the seams sometimes rub on your legs. You may want to consider getting Jodhpurs or breeches.
► Make sure your footwear is sturdy and has a decent heel so your foot won't go all the way through the stirrup. This way if you accidentally fall off, your foot won't get stuck in the stirrup.

3 Did you know that horses communicate with their heads and hindquarters? An angry horse will often put her ears back and show the whites of her eyes. If you see this type of expression, watch out.

4 A common misconception is that ponies are young horses. This is not true. There are three basic types of horses:
► A pony stands 10 to 14—2 hands (1 hand = 4 inches) and weighs between 300 and 850 lbs. Ponies are generally defined as small horses. The best known pony is the Shetland pony.
► A light horse stands 14—2 to 17 hands and weighs 800 to 1,300 lbs. Light horses are used for riding, racing, pulling light vehicles and ranch work.
► A draft horse stands 15—2 to 19 hands and weighs 1,500 to 2,600 lbs. Draft horses are used for pulling heavy loads and for farm labor. Medieval knights used them because their armor was so heavy. The best known draft horse is probably the Clydesdale.

Pet Tips: Our Fine Feathered Friends

THE PIRATE'S PET OF CHOICE AND PERHAPS YOURS AS WELL, IS THE BIRD. WHETHER IT'S THEIR SWEET SINGING, THEIR BEAUTIFUL FEATHERS OR THEIR COMPANIONSHIP YOU LIKE, BIRDS CAN EASILY BECOME BELOVED MEMBERS OF YOUR FAMILY.

1 LIKE RODENTS, FISH AND REPTILES, BIRDS NEED A SAFE AND SECURE PLACE TO LIVE. PAPER-LINED CAGES WITH A PLENTIFUL SUPPLY OF GOOD FOOD AND WATER ARE VERY IMPORTANT AND CAN EASILY BE PURCHASED AT YOUR LOCAL PET STORE.

2 TO MAKE SURE YOUR BIRD STAYS HEALTHY, FEED IT A PROPER DIET. A BALANCED DIET CONTAINS INGREDIENTS FROM ALL THE MAJOR FOOD GROUPS. A SEED-ONLY DIET LACKS MANY NUTRIENTS AND LEADS TO MALNUTRITION, POOR FEATHERS, INCREASED SUSCEPTIBILITY TO ILLNESS, AND A SHORTENED LIFE. PROCESSED PELLET FOODS, FRUITS, VEGETABLES, CEREALS, BREADS, AND PROTEINS LIKE BEANS, EGGS, OR MEATS SHOULD BE OFFERED TO PROVIDE A WELL-BALANCED DIET. AND CLEAN, FRESH WATER ALWAYS MUST BE AVAILABLE.

3 DID YOU KNOW THAT BIRD CHIRPING IS BELIEVED TO BE A KIND OF LANGUAGE? DIFFERENT SOUNDS HAVE DIFFERENT MEANINGS, AND THE WAY THEY'RE MADE WILL TELL YOU WHAT KIND OF BIRD IT IS. SOME BIRDS, LIKE MOCKINGBIRDS, MYNAS, LYRE BIRDS, AND PARROTS, ARE AWESOME MIMICS, AND CAN IMITATE MANY SOUNDS, INCLUDING HUMAN SPEECH. SO MAKE SURE YOU DON'T SAY ANYTHING MEAN ABOUT YOUR LITTLE BROTHER OR SISTER IN FRONT OF YOUR PARROT!

4 IMPORTANT TIP: EVEN THOUGH BIRDS ARE TERRIFIC COMPANIONS, DON'T KEEP THEM IN THE KITCHEN. THIS ISN'T BECAUSE THEY DON'T LIKE TO EAT, IT'S BECAUSE SOME KINDS OF NON-STICK COOKWARE EMIT AN ODOR WHICH COULD BE TOXIC TO THEM.

Dear best friend...

IF MY BEST FRIEND COULD UNDERSTAND ME, THIS IS WHAT I WOULD TELL HIM/HER (WRITE A LETTER).

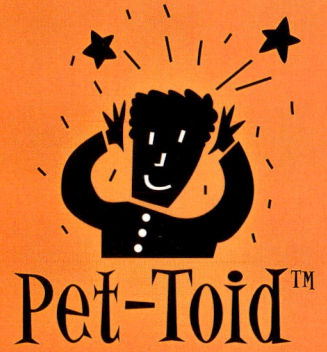

_____

_____

_____

_____

_____

_____

_____

_____

_____

_____

_____

_____

_____

_____

_____

_____

Pet-Toid™

HERE'S HOW TO

SAY "CAT" IN TEN

DIFFERENT LANGUAGES:

SPANISH - GATO

GERMAN - KATZE

ITALIAN - GATTO

DUTCH - KAT

FRENCH - CHAT

POLISH - KOT

GREEK - KATA

RUSSIAN - KOSHKAS

CHINESE - MAO

JAPANESE - NEKO

HAPPY 1st BIRTHDAY!

TODAY IS MY BEST FRIEND'S BIRTHDAY!

HEIGHT: _____

WEIGHT: _____

LENGTH: _____

HOW WE CELEBRATED: _____

_____

_____

_____

_____

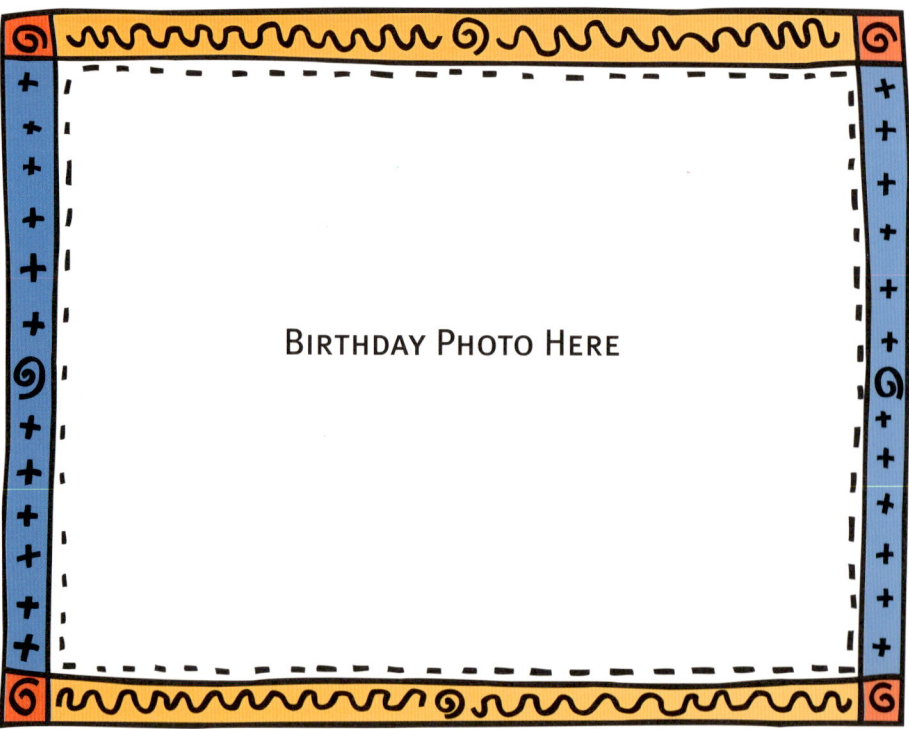

BIRTHDAY PHOTO HERE

HAPPY 2nd BIRTHDAY!

TODAY IS MY BEST FRIEND'S BIRTHDAY!

HEIGHT: _____

WEIGHT: _____

LENGTH: _____

HOW WE CELEBRATED: _____

_____

_____

_____

_____

BIRTHDAY PHOTO HERE

Pet-Toid™

THE OLDEST ANCESTOR OF THE HORSE IS THE EOHIPPUS, AND IT WAS ABOUT THE SIZE OF A COMMON HOUSE CAT. NOW WHERE WOULD YOU FIND A JOCKEY SMALL ENOUGH TO RIDE THAT HORSE, LET ALONE GETTING A SADDLE?

HAPPY 3rd BIRTHDAY!

TODAY IS MY BEST FRIEND'S BIRTHDAY!

HEIGHT: _____

WEIGHT: _____

LENGTH: _____

HOW WE CELEBRATED: _____

_____

_____

_____

_____

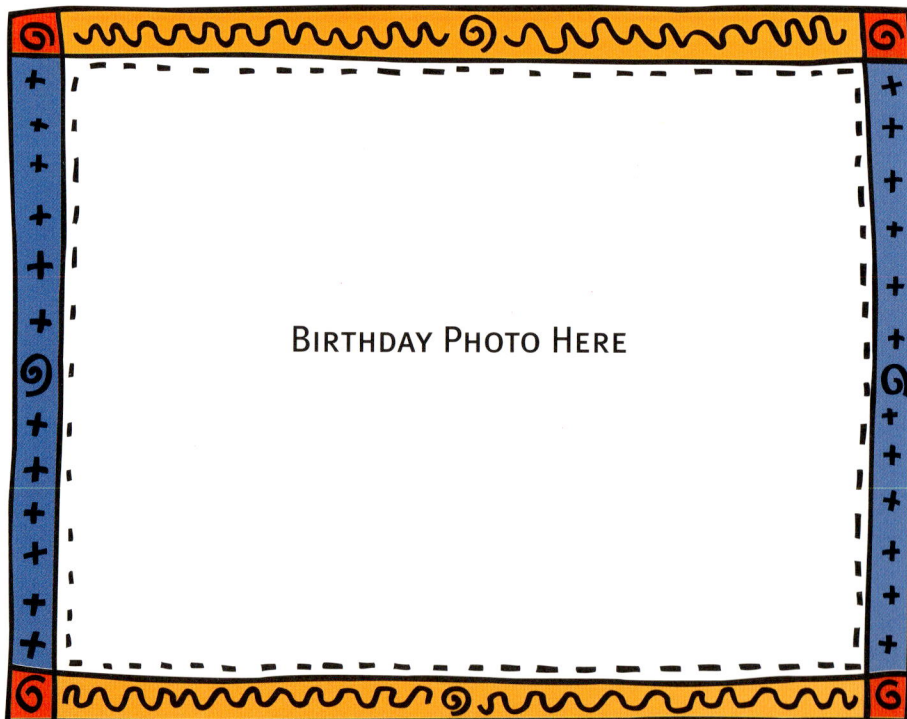

BIRTHDAY PHOTO HERE

HAPPY 4th BIRTHDAY!

TODAY IS MY BEST FRIEND'S BIRTHDAY!

HEIGHT: _____

WEIGHT: _____

LENGTH: _____

HOW WE CELEBRATED: _____

_____

_____

_____

_____

BIRTHDAY PHOTO HERE

HAPPY 5th BIRTHDAY!

TODAY IS MY BEST FRIEND'S BIRTHDAY!

HEIGHT: _____

WEIGHT: _____

LENGTH: _____

HOW WE CELEBRATED: _____

_____

_____

_____

_____

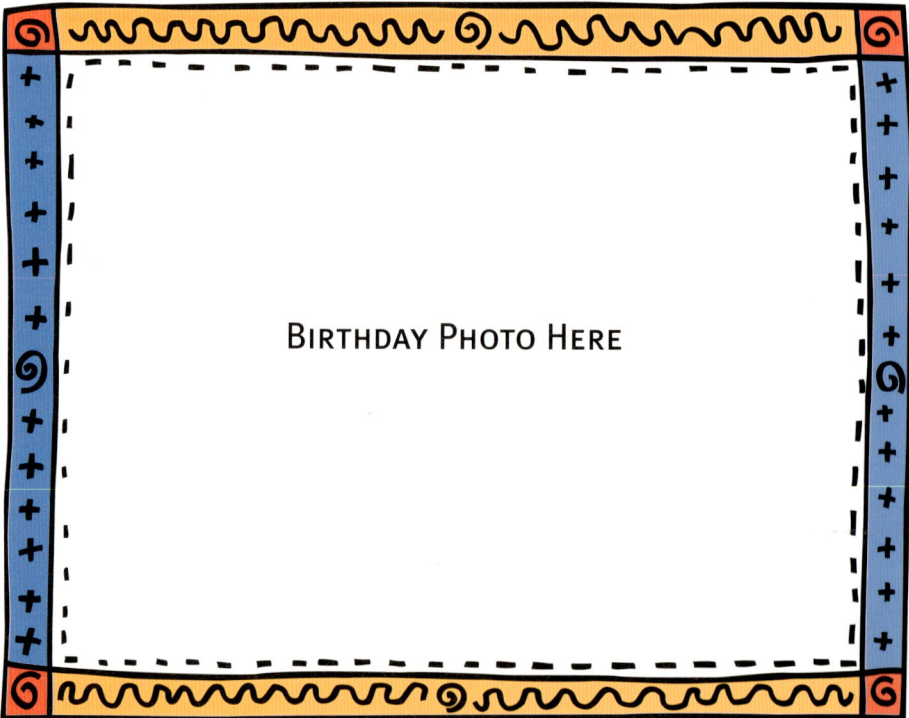

BIRTHDAY PHOTO HERE

HAPPY 6th BIRTHDAY!

TODAY IS MY BEST FRIEND'S BIRTHDAY!

HEIGHT: _____

WEIGHT: _____

LENGTH: _____

HOW WE CELEBRATED: _____

_____

_____

_____

_____

BIRTHDAY PHOTO HERE

HAPPY 7th BIRTHDAY!

TODAY IS MY BEST FRIEND'S BIRTHDAY!

HEIGHT: _____

WEIGHT: _____

LENGTH: _____

HOW WE CELEBRATED: _____

_____

_____

_____

_____

_____

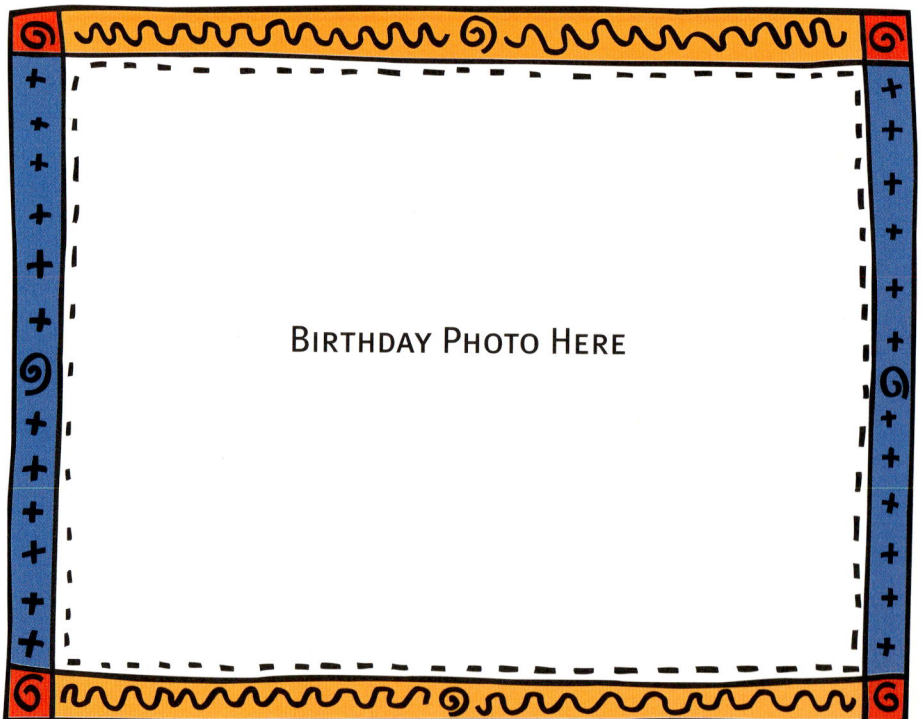

BIRTHDAY PHOTO HERE

HAPPY 8th BIRTHDAY!

TODAY IS MY BEST FRIEND'S BIRTHDAY!

HEIGHT: _____

WEIGHT: _____

LENGTH: _____

HOW WE CELEBRATED: _____

_____

_____

_____

_____

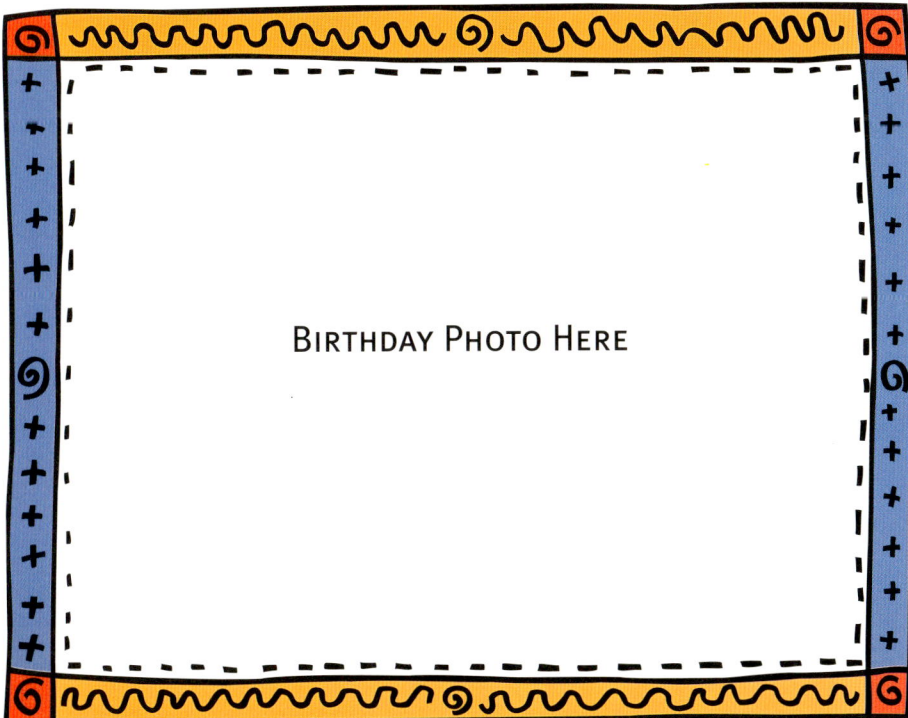

BIRTHDAY PHOTO HERE

Pet-Toid™

KANGAROOS HAVE HOPPED

INTO THE HEARTS

OF MANY AUSTRALIAN

PET-OWNERS. BUT,

SINCE THEY CAN HOP

AT SPEEDS OF UP TO

40 MILES PER HOUR,

YOU'D NEED TO TAKE

YOURS FOR A RUN,

NOT A WALK!

HAPPY 9th BIRTHDAY!

Today is my Best Friend's Birthday!

Height: _____

Weight: _____

Length: _____

How we celebrated: _____

_____

_____

_____

_____

Birthday Photo Here

HAPPY 10th BIRTHDAY!

TODAY IS MY BEST FRIEND'S BIRTHDAY!

HEIGHT: _____

WEIGHT: _____

LENGTH: _____

HOW WE CELEBRATED: _____

_____

_____

_____

_____

BIRTHDAY PHOTO HERE

FUN FILLED
PHOTO GALLERY

PLACE PHOTO HERE

PLACE PHOTO HERE

NOTES:

_____

_____

_____

_____

_____

_____

_____

_____

FUN FILLED
PHOTO GALLERY

PLACE PHOTO HERE

PLACE PHOTO HERE

FUN FILLED
PHOTO GALLERY

PLACE PHOTO HERE

PLACE
PHOTO
HERE

PLACE
PHOTO
HERE

PLACE PHOTO HERE